# twist

photography inspiring poetry

By Antoinette LeCouteur and Peter Dudley

Published by Gray Bear Publications, an imprint of
Gray Bear Coaching, LLC
2120 Contra Costa Blvd #1021, Pleasant Hill, CA 94523
graybearpublications.com

ISBN: 979-8-9876637-3-8

Gray Bear

Publications

# dedication

For you, you wonderful person, you.
Also for Alice.

# introduction

Welcome to a new perspective on the ordinary.

As artists, we want to view mundane, familiar things from a new perspective, reshape and twist them, and give them back to you in a way that inspires feeling: delight, rage, amusement, surprise, insight, learning.

In this book we do that, and then we do it again. Photographs, poems, and pairings. Layers entwined.

Antoinette captures moments from everyday life in photographs taken with her phone. These are found moments, not artistically and intentionally staged. She doesn't stay up all night to catch the moon in exactly the right spot over the mountain.

Instead, she notices the curious way that chairs have been haphazardly pushed to the side in a small restaurant. Or the contrast between two glasses of ice water.

Peter looks at each of these pictures and sees beyond the chairs and the glasses. He pulls on each thread of feeling and meaning that the photo inspires, then winds a new story from it in verse. That's how the chairs become a story about the transition of death, and the water glasses become a tale about two experiences of a single blind date.

When the poem and photo are paired, they create a third experience. The photo takes on new meaning from the poem, and the poem draws meaning from the picture. We did this in our first book, *together*, and we continue it in this book.

But this time we added a few twists.

This time Peter provided one of the photos, and Antoinette wrote the poem. In another week, Peter's poem inspired the picture that Antoinette provided.

The title also reflects the work it took to get this book created. When we made *together*, we did one pairing each week during 2022. But 2023 had some unexpected twists in store for us.

We said goodbye to our 17-year-old cat, Alice. We temporarily relocated across the country for a few months. We each had new successes and challenges in our professional lives. We met dozens of new, interesting, wonderful people. And our lives were disrupted again and again.

As we charge into 2024, we know more twists and turns are in store for us all. The act of playful creation is an important part of who we are and who we want to be. Life is rich, fulfilling, challenging, difficult, exhausting, surprising, delightful, full of color and light and magic. It's also far too short.

And that's why we hope that in addition to enjoying our art, you make time for creating your own art. The world needs more art, and it needs your unique twist on reality.

Whether you plan on publishing something or not, the act of creation is itself a worthy pursuit. We hope you feel inspired by this collection.

Peter & Antoinette

# Inspiration

In the dull purgatory of beige
Under a fluorescent glow
The only shadow cast
Is the doom of a creeping sameness
Pressing my thoughts
Until all creativity drains out
The way apples get pressed into mash
The color of skin
After all the life has drained out
Day after diluted day
I feel the hours slip by
And sometimes I think of
That snowy night in Chicago
Celebrating Judith's retirement
At the Peruvian restaurant
When we sang show tunes
In a neon green taxi
With too many drunk coworkers
And your rainbow scarf
Flowing out from under
Your chestnut hair
Danced its ticklish fringe
On the back of my hand

Week 1

# If You Come Back

It's just a line of trees, you said
And no one ever returns, I said
But you didn't hear the words
And I told myself that was because
My face was pressed so hard
Against your flannel-armored chest
I wanted my tears to soak in
To salt their way through the cloth
To bore into your skin
To mix with your blood
Take root in your heart
So one day if you ever did return
You would carry back to me
The last evidence that
I ever cared
About anything

Week 2

# Triplets

It's birthday time! We're turning eight!
All three of us, this special date.
It's just next week. We cannot wait.
And that's why we don't hesitate
To spy on mom so we'll locate
The presents she'll accumulate.
Last year she hid them in a crate.
This year, who knows? Let's speculate!
Perhaps beneath a dinner plate
Or in a box that's labeled "freight"
Or underneath a sewer grate
Or maybe in the Bering Strait
Or on the Bleathermans' estate.
But wait, what's this? Behind this gate!
It's yellow tissue paper, great!
Abuzz, we now anticipate.
We have you now, dear mom… checkmate!
But when we reach our *real* birthdate
We'll do our best to simulate
Surprise as we all celebrate!

# Rings

Squeeze your eyes
Until all the bridges you can see
Bend into a kaleidoscope illusion

Build a ring around time
No beginning, no ending
Observe from a safe distance
As shadows pinch the air
And the trembling refractions
Of opportunities scorned
Simulate the sensations of living

Compress your life
Let the days seep out
Like sap down the bark
Of a wounded tree

Week 4

# On Finding an Old Photograph

You said goodbye
In black and white
Your voice grainy
Like old film
The scenery melting away
In sepia streaks
As if a paperboy
Should be shouting
Out the news
Or a Greyhound bus should
Rumble patiently nearby
We left that place
In perpendiculars
Dressed in naiveté
Overflowing with ambition
Eager to create legacies

And now we've collided
At this sharp moment
Our imperfect reunion
In need of a little glue
And acceptance
To smooth over the cracks
And misalignments
That make it so hard
To smile for the camera.

Week 5

# Wingman

Remember the hills
That used to rise
Above the river
Brown and cracked
Like bread forgotten in the oven
They now lie decorated
With gaudy mini mansions
As if the old baker sold out
To an entrepreneur whose cakes
Would taste of new paint
If they tasted like anything at all

Remember the tobacco fields
Between the seasons
Traipsing over the cracked brown
Kicking dirt clods into dirt clouds
Imagining magnificent futures
Waving to the ancient farmers
Who rattled along
Atop their faded red tractors
They seemed as old as the soil
And just as dry and furrowed

Those were the days of possibility
When an empty horizon
Was an invitation to dream
When history rose up with the dust
Awakened by each sunburned step
Thick with the echoes of
Other people's ancestors
Guiding our imaginations
With the unshakable
Childhood certainty
Of permanence

Week 6

# Peekaboo

Heather McTethers would carry some feathers
No matter the weather outside.
She felt so afraid, she stalled and delayed,
And always she wanted to hide.
Til one day her father, who felt it a bother,
Commanded she leave them inside.
"You don't understand," she tried to demand,
"I can't, though I really have tried."
He then raised his voice and gave her no choice.
Reluctantly, then, she complied.
She tried not to pout when next they went out
Her anxiousness all held inside.
Then someone went by and tried to say hi
And Heather felt awful tongue-tied.
So up her hands flew. She yelled "peekaboo!"
And fell down, pretending she died.

# Creation

Hunched over his workbench

He hesitates

Peering through layered lenses
With bristled eyebrows quivering
As if undecided whether they should
Grind into the ancient ancestral scowl
Or lift in childish amusement

He ponders the result of his last stroke
A swooping arc curled at the end
With a particularly inexpert flourish
That only an infinity of luck
Or an infinity of skill
Could bring into existence

His shoulders sag under the weight of eons
The wrap of his shop-worn apron
Blending at the fringe into the leather of his skin
The wrinkles worn away long ago

And as his knobbed hand hovers
He senses the planets watching
He feels the vibrations of metals
He perceives colors stretching into the distance
And he understands that time has stopped for him

If it ever existed at all

Week 8

# Floodwaters

They built a fence, the old ones
The ones who scowl into their lemonades
The ones who long for simpler times
The days of Walter Cronkite
Now there was a real newsman
He told you the way it was
But dear old Uncle Ironpants never had a choice
He was a virtuoso in a world with two notes
A maestro in a world with two colors
A world where whales didn't yet need saving
And every villain spoke Russian
Where baseball, apple pie, and Chevrolet
Were as American as Old Glory itself
And no one important had yet noticed
That the waters were rising

They built a fence, the old ones
With split boards and iron nails
And good, sturdy posts dug deep into the earth
But the world has never known a fence
That can hold back the flood waters
And as temperatures and sea levels rise
The people rise with it
Inevitability seeps through
And when the revolution comes
Uncle Walt will look down from wherever
And with a contented smile he will say
That's the way it is

Week 9

# Legacy

Tear away the skin of the Earth
Rend soil from root
Pound living things to sand
Claw and gouge with ruthless grit
Until her veins lie defenseless
Streaks of dust-dry blood
Scrape out the ageless ore
Cart it to the forge and fire the furnace
Mix it with the sweat of laborers
Pour and shape it
Watch it rise skyward
Girder by beam
A tower bearing your name
Made of steel and glass and violence
But as you marvel at your legacy
The planets glide past overhead
And even as you turn to the cameras
Boastful of your self-made immortality
Corrosion begins to set in
Microscopic decay
For the Earth is patient
And she will reclaim her own
For even she knows her time is short
And one day the stars will forget her
Long after you and your glorious creation
Have been returned to nameless dust

Week 10

# Etchings

A decade ago
Beside the hearth in a mountain cabin
With autumn twilight dimming the windows
You scratched your flinted fingertips
Across the tempered steel of my heart
And rekindled a flame
That I thought had died long before
In the morning you said goodbye
And I stood on the rough-hewn porch
Watching your minivan kick up dust
From the unpaved driveway
Watching autumn dissolve into winter

Season after season
The dust from other strangers' cars
Clouded my view from the rough-hewn porch
The gritty grime of their passage
Swirling to settle on my numbing heart
Covering over your enduring scratches
A fine film mudded by the dews of spring
Baked hard under summer's unrelenting sun
Until after a decade of autumns
I linger lonely on my porch
And day by day it gets harder to see
Through the gathering soot

# Cotton Hollow

By the end of July
The towels
Washed pale by chlorine and sunshine
Had given up their rainbow stripes
And we
The coppery children
Exiled from the community pool
During the hour of Adult Swim
Snatched them up
Slung them across our necks
And flowed into the forest
On bare feet leathered
By the sizzling concrete summer
And I knew you'd get to the brook first
Dancing and leaping from root to rock
Unconcerned with the prickers and pebbles
I watched you
A forest sprite
Magic in your laughter
Shadowed under the spindly birch
You paused at the precipice
Looked back with exhiliration
Shouted "see you at the bottom"
And plunged

# Anchored

Take me with you
Out beyond the whale fields
Where spitting mists punctuate the morning
Ephemeral exclamation points
Among the rhythms of rising and rolling

Take me with you
Past the comforting shallows
Out to the azure deep
To gaze down into mystery
As we drift toward unknowns
On a woven raft of sailor's yarn

Take me with you
When twilight sighs its last
And our heartbeats match the waves
And you slide from daydream to nightdream
To sail among the impossibilities
Of a universe without end

# Wild Wonderful World
## Cabo San Lucas, Mexico

Week 13

# Revolutions

The revolution pauses
As the weary faces
Battered by age and toil
Grind on rusted gears
To squint at the haze
Of cigarette smoke and fear
Suspended
Above the exposed dance floor

Grumbled words tumble
Unheeded in the shadows
Discarded
Like artists' brushes
And musical instruments
Along the mudded roads

And we sit like statues
Watching the spotlights
Search the floor in arcs

The conductor
Cracks his baton
Music rises from the wings
The girl twirls into the light
Her dress
As orange as freedom
Glowing like liquid fire
An invitation to burn

And when the song ends
We in the dark corners
Our empty glasses refilled
Return to our sharp words
To talk again of beating
Our rusted plowshares
Into vengeful swords.

Week 14

# Eggshell White

maybe this time
you thought
maybe this time you wouldn't
end up crying in the car
tears and snot salting your lips
desperation smearing your cheeks
which you painted eggshell white
just like you painted your house
just like you painted your bedroom
just like you painted your personality
the perfect camouflage
so no one can see the weird beautiful you
which you keep hidden away
beside the remnants of yesterday's dreams

Week 15

# Deadname

When I told you I'd rather die
Than wear this stupid rental tux
You clucked and said "Oh Brad"
And fussed with the boutonniere
Declaring yet again how its pink petals
Would match Rebecca's dress to perfection
How we'd make the most stunning couple
It was only for one night after all
But the photos would last forever
You chose not to hear me screaming inside
As you laced your fingertips together
Clutching the ghosts you'd lost
And I realized then that it was never about me
I was just here to fill the clothes you chose
So I let you finish dressing me
Like readying a corpse for the viewing
And I smiled through the numbness
While you gathered photographic evidence
And then Rebecca and I drove away
And at the Texaco by the fourth street onramp
We ditched the tux in the bushes
Rebecca zipped me into her backup dress
And said we made the most stunning couple
And we hit the highway
Because if we're gonna die we'll do it our way
And you know we're all gonna die
Someday

Week 16

# As the Light Fades

When all the fat little birds line up together
Their tiny talons clenched tight to the telephone line
Bobbing and swaying in the evening breeze
And drop their chirpy little insults
Onto the heads of the heedless squirrels below

When the years we piled unsteadily in the corner
Lean slowly to the side then topple without a sound
Sink through the quicksand floor
Dragging with them the last of the stolen hours
To disappear in a puff of memory

When you lie on the cushioned couch
And the medicine seeps into your veins
All that's left to do is wrap you in a blanket
And gently cradle you in my arms
And listen to the beating of my own heart
As the sun sets for you
One last time.

Week 17

# Where the Clouds End

wandering the parched trail
beneath the pressing arms
of oak trees crooked and gray
sagging under an unnamed grief
and thick with the salted sea air
I carried a knapsack
heavy with other people's expectations
your voice startled me
like a rabbit springing from the tall grass
you lifted the knapsack from my shoulders
held it above your head
look up you said
and with a gust of wings
a raven swept from the sun
snatched away the pack
and carried off my burdens
across the widening fields
over the curving horizon
out to where the clouds end

Week 18

# Generations

now gather the cushions
and draw up the blanket
welcome the evening breeze
drifting across the garden
let the memories wink like fireflies
open our imaginations with tales of a fearless life
leave us breathless and threadbare
with the sparks you strike
wavering skyward
into the mysterious void
for we walk in our
unblossomed youth
bright
hungry
wishing
for wings
like yours

Renew
Walnut Creek, California

Week 19

# No One Knows

Pretend you don't see me
Sitting here in the shadow of the camellia
Under the weathered lamp post
At the bend in the river walk
Where crows gather secrets in twitchy silence
And history hisses unhearable memories
Like clandestine static
On an underground radio
Ignore the aromas of algae and mud
Rising from the torpid water
Thick with decaying leaves
And forgotten stories
Simply flow past with the tourists
In their short pants and sunburns
Carry on with your errands
As if I don't exist
For no one knows I used to be
King of the world
And I sit in silent patience
With my cane of rosewood and mahogany
Lying peaceful across my linen-lined lap

Arrived
Alexandria, Virginia

Week 20

# Pinwheels

Arriving at the fairground was always magical
Bumbling along in the old yellow bus
To tumble out at the top of a familiar slope
Breathing deep the smells of autumn hay and fried dough
Peering through the dust and jostling bodies
Trying to glimpse the ferris wheel and carnival games
Holding on to every ticket like it was pure gold
It's curious to think back now nearly five decades later
The melodies and colors fade to monotones
Detail gets diluted but the feelings have sharpened
And the parts I remember best
Aren't the rides or the games or the pinwheel toys
But I remember best the things I knew you loved
Sitting on the hillside watching oxen haul concrete blocks
Weaving through stalls full of goats and pigs
Marveling at the unbelievably gigantic pumpkins
And if I sit still and concentrate
I can almost hear the tractors grunting
At the far end of the field
As we trudge back up the trampled slope
Your hand wrapping mine in the darkening twilight

Week 21

# Enchantments

stand at that place where the cat used to sleep
rest your fingertips on the peeling paint
count the shadows that slant across your hand
listen for the sounds that are not yet forgotten
Great Aunt Kate humming a tune from the thirties
her knitting needles clicking like a broken metronome
while cabinets creak in the kitchen
amid the clatter of wooden spoons and rolling pins
the misrhythms of the morning harmonizing
as if the gods themselves pause behind you
arms crossed and heads tilted in scolding
it's the most beautiful of mornings
why are you not already playing outside?

Week 22

# Free Solo

letting go is not an option
clinging to hope
in fingertip desperation
alone
in the echoless void
collect courage in your gut
coil your soul
cinch it down
tight as you can
inhale the mistless void
savor the burn in your nostrils
reach out with your feelings
spy that next foothold
one more push upward
inch by excruciating inch
driven by faith
because at this point
it's either let go
or reach the top
and letting go
is not an option

Week 23

# Grandma's Pond

The blow-up raft lies forgotten in the barn
Crumpled in the creaky shadows with more than one pinhole leak
And more than one spider living in its folds and creases
The fishing rods sag against the wall
Their tangled lines hanging loose
Synthetic sinews woven through gossamer cobwebs
A cozy blanket of dust covers it all like an early snow
But out beyond the meadow
Over the rise where the crabapple tree stands guard
Past the woodchuck burrows and blackberry bushes
Grandma's pond lazes in the sunshine
Reflecting on all the summer swims and winter skating
And all the dragonflies chased and tadpoles caught
And maybe this summer when we go to the farm
We can drag out the folding chairs
Bring along some crackers and a bottle of wine
Listen to the hum of the bees in the wildflowers
Smell the lilac and rose and forest loam
Set our shoes on the flat rock
Wiggle our toes in the cool water
And remember all the laughter of seasons past.

Breathing Room
Morrisville, Vermont

Week 24

# I Got Here First

I'm just over here hangin' out
Don't pay me no never-mind
I'm sorry if I got in your photo
I didn't mean nothin' by it
But this flower smells so sweet
And I got here first
Before the sunrise actually
You shoulda seen the dew
Sparkling like diamonds
When the sun came over the hill
Then whoo the petals opened up
What a ride I'll tell you
And I'm sorry if you want me to move
But I'm stayin' right here until sunset
Maybe even til the stars come out
Because life is beautiful man
And the world is beautiful
And everything is beautiful
And you should stop a bit
Y'know just stop
And smell the flowers
And taste the dew
And gaze at the stars
Or take a picture I dunno
And save it on your computer
And never look at it again
Anyway
I got here first

Week 25

# The Last Drop

I know I know I know I know!
We really really have to go.
You've said it once, you've said it twice.
But nagging isn't very nice.
No need to rush! No need to run.
I promise that I'm almost done.
So let me be!
Don't make me stop.
Just let me

get

this

one

last

drop.

Week 26

# Shipwreck

in the lengthening hours
when your heart tumbles on the ebbing tide
and thoughts wither as the day becomes dust
turn away from the flashing gold
that beckons from the hill forsaken
match your course to the sea birds
lash yourself to the mast, dear friend
listen beyond the creaking timbers
to the wisdom of the weeping wind
and heed not the false seduction
that has lured so many to ruin

# On the Horizon

Get down the hill mama
Before the lightning comes
Can you feel the air get sharp
Like needles in your hair
The leaves have all gone gray
And the soil trembles so
Please mama get down the hill
Don't linger in your daydream
On the naked granite peak
Lost in foolish fantasy
Dreaming of a heaven
That was never meant for you
Put on your shoes now
And button up that dress
And get down the hill now mama
Before the lightning comes

Week 28

# Bland Date (part 1)

Mister Bland showed up at eight,
His trousers pressed, his tie on straight,
Not sure what to anticipate
Or if Miss Ice would show up late.
Miss Ice, it seemed, had got there first.
Her arms were crossed; her lips were pursed.
And Bland thought, "This will be the worst!"
He felt his dating life was cursed.
He tried to make the evening light
But couldn't seem to get it right.
She peppered him all through the night—
Interrogating left and right.
Her questions were both rude and bold.
Her frosty gazes made him cold.
He hoped he soon would be paroled,
But still he kept himself controlled.
And in the end, the evening spent,
He found the end of his torment.
He couldn't hide his discontent.
With frozen heart, away he went.

# Last Night
Boston, Massachussetts

Week 29

# Bland Date (part 2)

Miss Ice, quite eager for a mate,
Agreed to go on one blind date.
She hoped, at least, she wouldn't hate
This guy who looked—on paper—great.
She'd tried so many times before,
With each attempt a useless chore.
When every man's a dreadful snore,
Just what did she do all this for?
Then here he came, all dressed in tan,
His skin the tone of marzipan,
His voice a shy and weak deadpan.
He seemed a dreadful, boring man.
She knew that first impressions lied,
And so all night she tried and tried.
She prodded, poked, cajoled, and pried.
His dullness left her glassy-eyed.
And in the end, the evening spent,
She found the end of her torment.
She couldn't hide her discontent.
Let down again, away she went.

# Motivations

I hop up one, then jump down two
Then up three more, and drop back four.
It seems no matter what I do
I always land right back with you.

With each advance and each retreat
I wonder what I do this for.
Why do I scamper this concrete?
It's cuz you always bring a treat.

# Hello Again
## Walnut Creek, California

Week 30

# Color-Safe Bleach

they say the grass is greener
and maybe that's how it seems to you
I hear it in your smothered sighs
wishing for clearer air to breathe
and your crumpled words
mismatched and threadbare
like old socks
I see it in the snapping glances
your patience worn out
shrunk tight with age
I feel it in your coarse touch
like stiff gardening gloves
tattered and faded
yet still mostly functional
the grass may be greener
my love
but even as you turn away
your loose gaze on the unknown
know that each time I look at you
the world bursts open
with so much color
that no amount of green
could steal my heart away

# Believe

She crouched and cowered
Shivering in the shadows cast
By the ones she looked up to
The ones who spoke in bright colors
The ones who danced loud
The ones who created stories
Rather than simply telling them
She wished
Oh how she wished
She could weave clouds in her hair
Shake hands with the sun
Taste the crisp blue of the sky
And she went on wishing
Until one day a voice fell
Like wet autumn leaves
It told her
Little one
We do not get courageous
By being big
We get big
By being courageous

Week 32

# Under the Armor

peel away the layers
in strips of crackling
stripe by ragged stripe
let them fall loose
like laughter in the rain
brush your ridged fingertips
along the shy grain exposed
and when the breeze stills
and the crickets start to doze
find the spirit inside
winking mischief at the world

Week 33

# Commute

you can't get a seat
on the train at four thirty
or even at five or half past six
the people seep out of buildings
in a monochrome ooze
exhaling relief and exhaustion
leaving behind undone tasks
and motivational paper weights
and someone else's dreams
they flow along the streets
and drain down stairwells
into the subway
stagger through the doors
lower their heads
lift their arms
grab the strap
and wait

Week 34

# Moving In

Well hi! Hello! How do you do?
It's great to meet somebody new.
I'm glad you're here. My name is Sue.
And over there's Bartholomew.
Together, we're the welcome crew
For this delightful rendezvous.
I love your avant-garde hairdo!
You'll have to tell me your shampoo!
And though this ain't Park Avenue
You'll love this place all through-and-through,
And we will love you right back, too.
So much, you might think we're cuckoo!
So cock-a-doodle-doodle-doo!
Our pleasure is to welcome you!

# Equality

when the mourners have gone
and the parking lot has emptied
when the janitor pauses at the light switch
and scans the room to find all the chairs
pushed roughly into corners
when the floor is swept clean
of soiled napkins and paper plates
and the flowers are crammed
blossom-first into compost bins
when the industrial fridge hums
a joyless dirge from the next room
it's then that the ghosts arrive
Shakespeare and Kennedy
Marie Curie and Valentino
Lau Tsu and Alfred and Joan
and every one of their neighbors
untold billions of souls
gathering at the edge of existence
waiting for the flick of the switch
waiting for the darkness
to reach through the timeless curtain
and welcome the newest member
to the club that lets everyone in

Week 36

# How do I get there from here

What's over there? she asked
A place where people live and love, I said
How do I get there? she asked
One step at a time, I said

Her small warm hand wriggled in mine
she snuggled closer to my leg against the wind

I looked down to her bright blue eyes peeking up at me
from a bundle of dark curls, trusting I would provide an answer

How do I get there from here? she asked
No one way, only your way, I said

Who is over there? she asked
Magic and Mayhem, I said

How will I know if I have met Magic or Mayhem? she asked

A good question my love but one I can't answer
You'll have to learn to trust your own instincts

She was quiet a moment, then pushed on
What do they look like? she asked
Like anyone, but I do know
Magic isn't always bright and shiny
Mayhem isn't always loud or angry

She dropped my hand, stepped forward,
pushed her face against the fence to get a closer look

She softly started singing
The song my mother sang while making bread
A song I hadn't heard since we left home
She stopped singing and without turning round
What am I? she asked
I scooped her up and hugged her close, burying my face in her curls
You my love are both
She hugged me tight and whispered,
just like you.

Week 37

# The Corner Table

there's two types
uncle Gino says
the regulars
and the phonies
he sips his peroni
the foam lingering
on his graying mustache
and I nod
not just because
that's what you do
when uncle Gino talks
but also because
I know what he means
as we wait in silence
our backs to the bar
to see which type
will come in to claim
aunt Cecilia's favorite table

Week 38

# Queen

Behold and despair
You peasants and peons
Look upon my grandeur
If you dare
Shrink into your pathetic smallness
Your drab plainness
Envy and worship me
For I am the infinity
And the glory
The like of which
Will never come again

Week 39

# Now is a Good Time

Now is a good time to visit the seagulls
Traipsing along the sand
Chasing the surf
Hunting hamburger buns clenched in the tiny fists of toddlers

Now is a good time to bake cookies
Sit nearby with a book and wait for the timer's chime

Now is a good time to gaze at the clouds because
Chances are they will never ever ever ever be exactly the same
As they are right now

Now is a good time to confront the blank page
Take up arms against its tyranny by uncapping a new pen
And create a new thing that has never existed before

Now is a good time
Now is the best time
Because when all the years are swept together
In a pile like dusty legos in the corner
And the clouds have moved on to Iowa
To amuse the lazy cows in their fields
And the color has drained from the ink
Take a moment to notice the setting sun
Imagine a person unknown to you far away
Looking up to notice the rising sun

Feel the untamed joy in this moment
Because now is a good time

Week 40

# Home Early

What hides there
behind this gray curtain
its folds ragged
as if drawn together
in a haste-harried
breathlessness
rumpled and cockled
much like the beige sheets
humped shapeless
on the floor
their testimony drowned
by white noise
from the bathroom
where you shower
satisfied
while I question
the whispering ghosts
impatient for justice
and in this gray moment
for the first time
I see my lines
once so sharply drawn
now blurred
and I slip quietly away
choosing one more
tomorrow

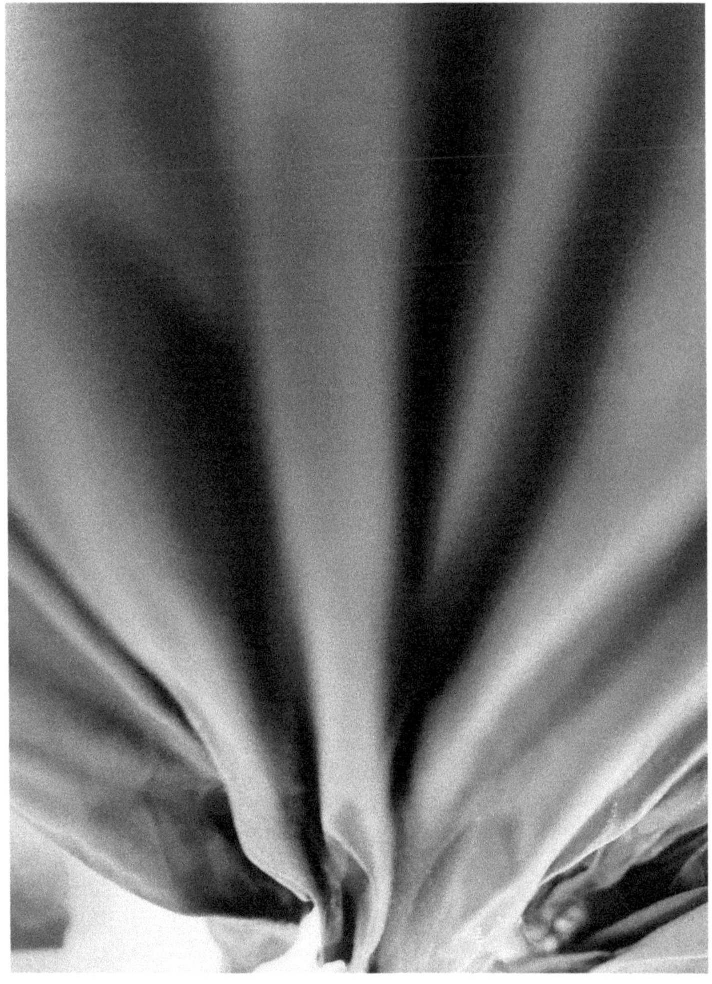

Week 41

# Summer's End

come brightly across the meadow
where ages forgotten
swell in the dewdrops
and the trembling blades
reveal the dancing of fairies
hopping and dodging
on the playful breeze
under the gentle applause
of golden leaves

Week 42

# Heads Will Roll

Be it resolved
That we of Good Conscience
Being Dedicated to the most proper Morality
And concerned only with the Welfare of All
Having Suffered unconscionable Ordeals and Ills
At the hands of the Tyrannical Oppressors
In the Spirit of establishing a Perpetual Harmony
Among all the Peoples of these Lands,
Filled with the Charity of God
And His unwavering Benevolence and Grace
Do hereby
Vow, promise, declare, and aver
That we shall perpetrate upon our Enemies
Unyielding and unrelenting Justice
With such Violence as may be necessary
To return this Country to its former glory
And place our Righteous and Benevolent Leader
Once more in the Seat of Power

Week 43

# Surprise

isn't it a nice rose color
I say without looking at her

isn't what a nice rose color
she asks from the couch
without looking up
freshly polished nails
clacking away at her phone
blue lipstick smeared
on the rim of her riesling
auburn hair freshly blown out
newly shaved legs tucked up

I pull the once-white sheet
from the dryer
still hot
pinch the corners
tuck under my chin
fold again
admire the subtle waves
pink, lavender, dusky rose

isn't physics marvelous
I say without looking at her

isn't what marvelous
she says without looking up

marvelous I say
that you did the laundry

oh she replies
you're welcome
I bought a new skirt she says

is it a red skirt I ask

uh huh how did you know

Week 44

# At the Business Conference

poolside on the hotel roof
my elbow draped on the metal rail
a warm breeze off the bay
goosebumps rising on bare shoulders
it was a difficult choice
the silver dress or blue
cut low or slit high
sleeveless either way

the neon city night is narrated
by bus engines and taxi horns
under the nervous murmur
of colleagues and competitors
boozed to the point of temptation
but afraid to test the waters

you slide into view
a warm breeze off the bay
floating and teasing
between the bodies
you drift to my side
your lips to my ear
I got your text you whisper
and my husband didn't come this year either

# Jump in, the Water is Fine
## Nashville, Tennessee

# Maybe Tomorrow

Even on this summer day
Beside the river
Her favorite park bench
Weathered by sun and rain
Seems a lonely place
For her grab-and-go lunch
A supermarket tuna salad
In a flimsy plastic box
With a flimsy plastic fork
Same as yesterday
Attractive people gallop past
In hundred-dollar leggings
Kicking up dust and gravel
Chasing aggressive goals
Or maybe fleeing a toxic past
It can be so hard to tell
When you're in the middle of it
She only knows she is suffocating
Like a chain around her neck
She wants to cut herself free
Run reckless to a new future
But she's afraid that if she does
She may by accident
Leave her heart behind
While the chain remains
Still tight around her throat

Week 46

# Everywhere

in the desert near that point
where California ends
and the casinos begin
a sand basin lies aglow
its floor paved with
a quarter million mirrors
each deflecting rays of light
hurled at the Earth
by the sun's nuclear violence
and all those tangled rays
bleach the air
a bubble of distortion
hot enough to flash-bake
the unfortunate wayward sparrow
while a thousand miles away
at the same moment
other rays of light
hurled by the same sun
create accidental art
worlds within worlds
reflected and refracted
in the tiny bubbles
floating in a city fountain
paved with blue tile

# Through the Window

In the drab pall of winter
When the stagnant air smothers joy
And the voices of children fall
To the dampened earth
Like the ashes of fireworks
I look to the fluttering wings
Of a hummingbird
Dodging through naked branches
Intrepid and defiant
And I imagine the colors and music and laughter
Of all those lost summer days
As I wrap my numbing fingers
Loose around my morning tea
Its wispy white steam swirling
A carousel of ghostly dreams

Week 48

# Illuminated

Can you remember a time
When there were no lights?
We lay on our backs in the frosty dirt
Shoes and jackets and mittens discarded
Fingers intertwined
Despair and grief reached up from the mud
Wrapped around our souls like vines
We welcomed the coming oblivion
Because we had each other
And then you saw that shooting star
Or at least you said you did
You flung your hand skyward and snatched it
Ran your fingers through my hair
"Someone sent that to us," you said
You pulled me up and led me home
And together we lit a single candle
And it was enough

Week 49

# The End

Follow me
You who ride upon comets
Forged in ice and stone
Steel-eyed and cold blooded
Scraping your slogans in the void

Follow me
You rank and ruthless heathens
Bloodthirsty barbarians clattering your swords
Full-throated and scarlet-maned
Crashing shields against the stars

Follow me
For I rise from the ashes
Of a burned and forsaken future
Where the damned dance and brawl
Beneath the braying of angels

Follow me
Through the ruin of ages
Through the death of suns
Through phantasm and nightmare
Until hope of victory is lost
In the ending of all ages

# Preschool Pickup

they cascade down the preschool steps
like candies tumbling from a gumball machine
a sticky cacophony of motion
spinning and bouncing in ricochets
loosely aimed at parents
who cut short their chattering
turn toward the deluge
spread their arms
and brace for impact

Week 51

# Mates for Life

I guess this pier
Is as good a place as any
To spend New Year's Eve
It's a beautiful evening after all
A bit chilly but at least there's no rain
Remember last year it rained
And we are together
Which is nice
I suppose
And the view is pleasant
With the setting sun
Shimmering on the water
And there's no one to bother us
Since they're all on the ferry
Enjoying the soft warm seats on the ferry
Drinking champagne on the ferry
Singing Auld Lang Syne on the ferry
And I really wouldn't mind so much
Missing the last ferry of the day
If you hadn't insisted so fervently
Just like last year
That it wasn't the last ferry

Week 52

# About The Photographs

**Week 1**  **Woven Together**

Walnut Creek, California
A blanket's rainbow-fringed edge twists on top of a
plain beige bed sheet.

**Week 2**  **Winter Sky**

Walnut Creek, California
A line of pine trees viewed from below, backed by
a blue blending into a pink sunset lit winter sky
behind the trees.

**Week 3**  **Room for All**

Walnut Creek, California
Three honeybees huddle in the center of a brilliant
yellow blossom.

**Week 4**      **After the Rain**

Walnut Creek, California
We look through three ceramic rings in a decorative
wall overlooking a creek with another bridge in the
background blurred.

**Week 5**      **Worn but Wise**

Walnut Creek, California
The lower left corner of a rough, wooden picture
frame against a gritty, tomato-red painted wall.

**Week 6**      **Sky Clearing**

Berkeley, California
Two seagulls soar in a dramatic, blue sky over the
San Francisco Bay.

**Week 7**      **Reach Up**

Walnut Creek, California
The curved leaves of a tropical plant stretch up
from the lower left, reaching up to the right into a
blue sky.

**Week 8**      **Seeing You Again**

Walnut Creek, California
What appears to be a monochrome, black-and-
white abstract pattern is actually a black metal table
covered in the water of an overnight rain, reflecting
the bare branches of a tree above.

**Week 9      Star Light**

Walnut Creek, California
Looking down the back side of a wooden gate at
the pavement, all lighted in unusually orange and
teal tainted lighting at twilight.

**Week 10      Crossings**

Walnut Creek, California
An orange-rust-colored metal girder is covered in
green and white lichens.

**Week 11      Looking**

Joshua Tree, California
The trunk of a Joshua tree twists up from the
ground, creating the illusion of an ancient, wizened
face.

**Week 12      Unfurling**

Walnut Creek, California
A closeup of a raindrop in the center of a purple
kale leaf, which is curled so it creates the effect of a
tube swirling down and away through the middle.

**Week 13      Wild Wonderful World Awaits**

Cabo San Lucas, Mexico
An iguana suns itself on top of a rock wall, looking
out over the Pacific Ocean on a sunny, warm, nearly
cloudless afternoon.

## Week 14    Crinkled Paper

Berkeley, California
A close-up of a bright orange California poppy in
full bloom with a field of more poppies blurred in
the background.

## Week 15    Pop of Color

Mount Diablo State Park, California
A butterfly stands on a lichen-covered rock, its
wings up. The outside of the wings are white with
black spots and orange highlight, and the inside are
dark blue.

## Week 16    Soft Rest

Walnut Creek, California
Two pink flowers lie on a pitted pavement.The one
in front is in focus; the one in the background is
torn apart, with petals scattered around.

## Week 17    Worn Beautifully

Walnut Creek, California
Close-up view of the petals and inner part of a
yellow flower, whose petals look like crepe paper.

## Week 18    New Horizons

Martinez, California
This picture shows a broad vista from the top of a
hill covered in tall grasses, under a brilliant blue
sky at midday.

Week 19    **Renew**

Walnut Creek, California
A red and black caterpillar traverses a thin filament
of a plant among its bright green leaves.

**Weary Beauty**

Walnut Creek, California
An old, black butterfly perches with threadbare
wings spread amid the purple flowers of a plant.

Week 20    **Arrived**

Alexandria, Virginia
A bird sits in silhouette on a wire atop a streetlamp
in the historic port district.

Week 21    **A Life Well Lived**

Hebron, Connecticut
The pale flowers of a dogwood highlight against its
dark green leaves.

Week 22    **A New Room, a New View**

Morrisville, Vermont
In a dark room, a dark wooden chair sits in front of
a window which looks out onto a brightly lit, green
yard with trees and a lawn.

**Week 23     How to Share a House**

Morrisville, Vermont
A large carpenter ant hangs on the underside of
a white curtain rod on a shower curtain with a
yellow wall in the background.

**Week 24     Breathing Room**

Morrisville, Vermont
Looking across a pond ringed with green trees,
mostly pines, reflected in the calm water.

**Week 25     Making New Memories**

Stowe, Vermont
A tiny, black beetle hides at the top of a petal on a
white peony blossom with pink highlights.

**Week 26     Pollen Pantaloons**

Morrisville, Vermont
A honeybee hangs upside-down with its head
inside the bell flower of an asparagus bloom and its
legs covered in pollen.

**Week 27     Gathering Sky**

Watch Hill, Rhode Island
A classic, old, white lighthouse with a red roof
sits lonely on a low, grassy hillside with the Long
Island Sound behind it on an overcast day.

**Week 28    Blue Sky After the Storm**

Stowe, Vermont
Looking up through vibrant green trees, we see a
blue sky textured with clouds in various shades of
sunlight and gray.


**Week 29    Last Night**

Boston, Massachussetts
From above, two water glasses sit touching side by
side on a black table. One glass  is filled with ice
water, and the other has a small amount of water at
the bottom, without ice.


**Week 30    Hello Again**

Walnut Creek, California
A squirrel stands attentively staring at the camera
on the middle step of a concrete staircase outdoors.


**Week 31    Summer Color**

Walnut Creek, California
A western honeybee climbs up and over the top of
a vibrant pink and yellow lantana blossom away
from us.


**Week 32    Sunrise**

Eugene, Oregon
A sunflower stands tall above us in silhouette
against a deep blue, cloudless sky. The sun shines
through the golden petals.

**Week 33**    **Patina**

Point Pinole, California
The trunk of a sycamore in closeup shows vertical
patterns of peeling bark, with a knot and a spot that
look slightly like the two eyes of a face hidden in
the wood.

**Week 34**    **Cooler in the Shade**

San Luis Obispo, California
Seen from above, the green-and-white striped
leaves of a plant crowd together as if reaching
upward toward the camera.

**Week 35**    **Hello Beautiful**

Avila Beach, California
A comically fancy chicken with fluffy, frilly black-
and-white feathers sticks her head into the picture
and looks inquisitively at the camera. In the
background, a fat white hen stands behind, blurred.

**Week 36**    **After They Leave**

San Luis Obispo, California
Six simple metal chairs sit empty, close together on
a beige linoleum floor, pushed up against a dark
gray wall in a small restaurant.

**Week 37    Excluded**

Alameda, California
Photo taken by Peter. Through two diamonds in
a chain-link fence we see across an abandoned
airstrip, then across the San Francisco Bay. In the
left diamond is the city of San Francisco in the
distance. In the right is the Bay Bridge.


**Week 38    Table for Two**

Las Vegas, Nevada
A brass table tent with the word "Reserved"
engraved in it sits in focus in the foreground on a
dark wood  restaurant table, with the background
scenery blurred.


**Week 39    Resilience**

Walnut Creek, California
A beautiful Monarch butterfly sits with wings
spread wide on a bit of lantana that is orange, red,
and yellow.


**Week 40    Drifting**

Morrisville, Vermont
Photo selected by Antoinette to match Peter's
poem. A small patch of the surface of a pond on a
windless day, with several stems of reed sticking up
on the left side and bright, fluffy clouds reflected on
the right side.

**Week 46    New Love**

Walnut Creek, California
A small, heart-shaped pendant sits in isolation in
the winter sunlight on a wooden bench.

**Week 47    Laughter**

Walnut Creek, California
A small, tight group of bubbles float atop the water
of a fountain in closeup. Inside each of the bubbles,
the blue tile mosaic of the fountain's bottom is
copied in miniature.

**Week 48    Flying**

Las Vegas, Nevada
A hummingbird with wings spread back is
alighting on the tip-top of a naked branch
among other branches, all in silhouette against a
monochrome desert sky.

**Week 49    Shine a Light for Everyone**

San Francisco, California
Looking up a leafless tree trunk from the ground,
we see colorful Christmas lights wrapping the tree
up into the distance, blurring as they go.

## Week 50   Fire Breathing Dragon

Walnut Creek, California
A creeper vine with bright read leaves stretches out
from the right side of the frame toward the left side,
with the vine looking like tendrils trailing to the
left.

## Week 51   Grayscale

Walnut Creek, California
Eucalyptus leaves and berries cascade to fill the
entire frame, with the trunk of the eucalyptus
peeking through the bottom part of the picture.

## Week 52   Two by Two

Walnut Creek, California
Two geese stand atop an office building, with
a blue sky in the background. One goose looks
away while the other appears to be looking at the
photographer.

# About Peter

Peter is an author and executive coach who tries to make the most of every day. He grew up in Connecticut with summers in Las Vegas, got his electrical engineering degree from UC Berkeley, then went on a long and winding career in startups, nonprofits, and big corporations. Once both his kids were grown, he started Gray Bear Coaching and Gray Bear Publications. Peter has published four novels and a chapter book, and his poetry, short fiction, and professional articles have been published in a wide array of journals and anthologies. Find him at peterdudley.com and graybearcoaching.com.

# About Antoinette

Antoinette is a consultant specializing in helping people do good in the world. A theatre major in college and actor early in her career, she transitioned to the world of philanthropy and social impact in the mid-2000s and has helped get hundreds of millions of dollars in employee donations and corporate funds to charities all over the world. In her photography, she captures moments that happen, rarely staging a photograph but preferring to see the world as it is, in unique ways and from new angles. She is especially fond of pollinators, and her camera roll is filled with bees, butterflies, and insects of all types going about their work of maintaining the world. Find her at CreateImpact.world.

# together

Antoinette and Peter's first book, *together*, is available for purchase wherever you buy books in paperback, hardcover, and ebook. Peter and Antoinette love to attend book groups, read at events, and sign reader copies. Find out more on the Gray Bear Publications website:

graybearpublications.com/books/together

## About Gray Bear Publications

In a world gone mad with commercialism and consumerism, we care more about beauty, wisdom, and humanity than fame or fortune. The Gray Bear represents strength, wisdom, independence, truth, reliability, and authenticity. Whether you're a poet or a spiritual guide, a photographer or a public speaker, a teacher or a grandma—if you've got something you want to say, we want to help you say it.

In addition to hybrid publishing, assisted self-publishing, collaborative books, and Gray Bear merchandise, we also offer book coaching and design services.

We invite you to learn more at graybearpublications.com.

# invitation

Because the world needs more art, we hereby invite you to create something new. Take a picture. Paint something! Write a poem, a story, or an opinion. Sing a song. Dance... alone or with others. Get it on video, or let it pass by like the sun in the sky.

Create something new that has never existed before. Share it with someone else, or keep it to yourself.

And if you feel so moved, tell us about it. Because the world needs more art. The world needs *your* art.